Land Company East Tennessee

Two years of Harriman

Tennessee

Land Company East Tennessee

Two years of Harriman
Tennessee

ISBN/EAN: 9783337113452

Printed in Europe, USA, Canada, Australia, Japan

Cover: Foto ©Andreas Hilbeck / pixelio.de

More available books at **www.hansebooks.com**

TWO YEARS of HARRIMAN TENN.

TWO YEARS OF

HARRIMAN

TENNESSEE.

Established by the

EAST TENNESSEE LAND COMPANY

February 26.
1890.

Designed, Illustrated, and Printed
by
THE SOUTH PUBLISHING CO.

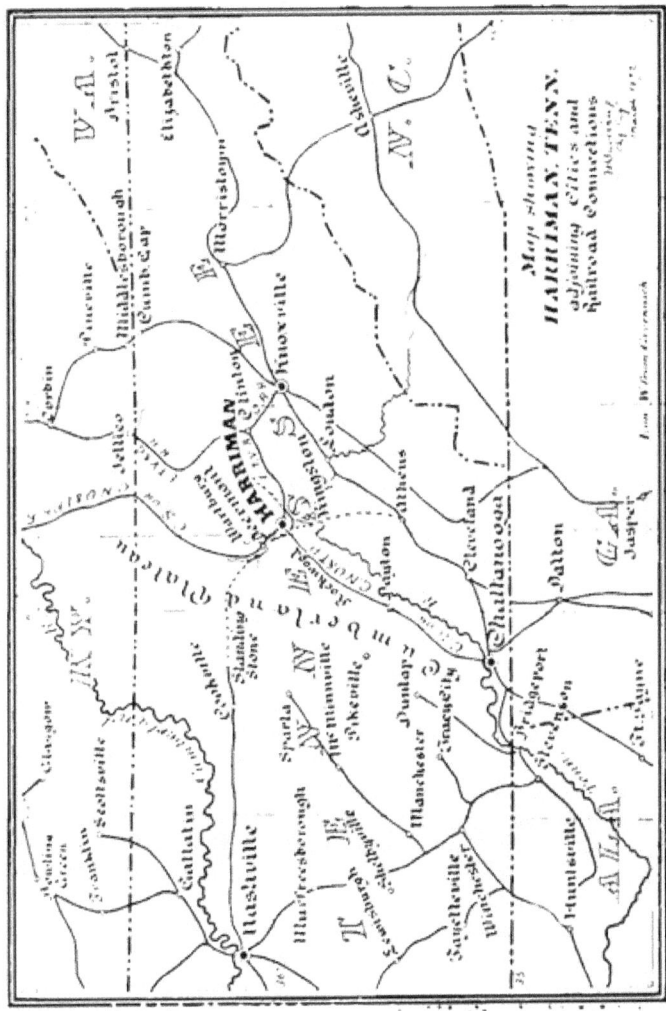

HARRIMAN

Knoxville

Bristol
Elizabethton
Morristown
Asheville
Clinton
Loudon
Athens
Cleveland
Chattanooga
Dalton
Jasper
Bridgeport
Stevenson
Huntsville
Nashville
Gallatin
Murfreesboro
Shelbyville
Tullahoma
Manchester
Winchester
McMinnville
Pikeville
Sparta
Crossville
Standing Stone
Monterey
Rockwood
Kingston
Middlesborough
Cumb. Gap
Pineville
Corbin
Williamsburg
Scottsville
Franklin
Bowling Green

V_a.
N. C.
Ga.
Ala.
Ky.
Tenn.
Cumberland Plateau

MAP OF
HARRIMAN
TENN.

Showing Railway River
& Road Connections
Scale

MORGAN   CO.

HARRIMAN   CO.

ROANE   CO.

Emory R.

Emory R.

Clinch R.

Tennessee R.

KINGSTON

Railroads
do Graded
do Surveyed
Wagon roads

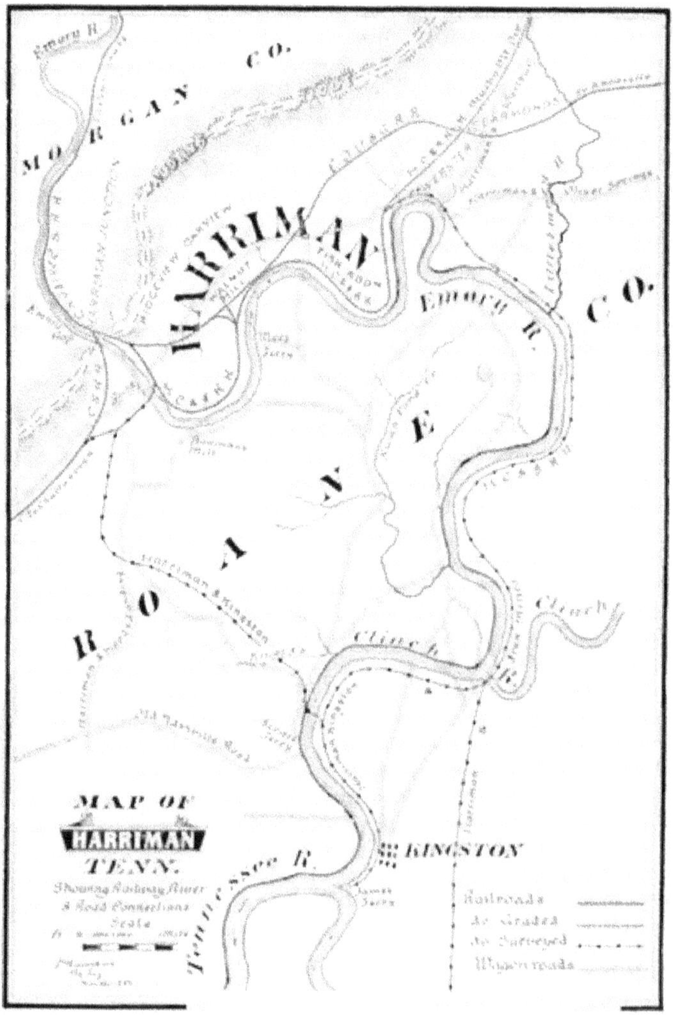

SECOND ANNIVERSARY VERSES.

[Read at the Birthday Celebration of Happy Harriman, in the W. C. T. U. Temple, Friday evening, Feb. 26, 1892.]

Two years! do they doubt it, who visit us here?
Does it seem as if time had stood still with each year?
Has a Joshua bidden the sun on its way
Here to linger, and leave us one marvelous day
With creation's own magic each moment to fill,
And the gift of creation each finger to thrill,
Until into some week full of wonder was wrought
Human hope, human faith, with Divinity's thought?

Be it so! From the morn beyond Emory's Heights.
To the evening, that glowed with her golden delights
Through the Gap in the west, what a day was our own
When our Joshua willed it! Sure never was known
Better service for men, of obedient sun!
Look about you, and see what creation has done
Where the hands of the willing, the hearts of the true,
At the breast of the Old have been nursing the New!

Here are homes where but yesterday nothing was built
Save the nests of the birds, on the branches atilt
Singing matins or vespers; and here on the slopes
There are altars erected, around which the hopes
Of glad households are gathered; here churches upraise
To the blue sky above us their eloquent praise;
And the work of creation goes on with a will,
As with hope and with faith marry courage and skill.

4

By the gleam of our forges are muscles of steel
Beating iron to gold ; the great steam hammers deal
Their unwearying blows on the masses below,
Till in beauty transformed, as in value, they glow
From our furnaces molten the liquid flames run,
As if here Tubal Cain his profession begun ;
In the mills and the factories Labor's delight
Is with muscle and brain to make glory of might '

Is it only two years ? or is time but a cheat,
And are we here assembled to help his decent ?
Do we dream that so late we were bold pioneers
Where a city thus active, progressive appears ?
From the corn-fields that blazoned their blades in the sun,
Have our faith and our works a great victory won ?
Is it true that our homes in their beauty have sprung
From the forest that sheltered the birds while they sang ?

Be your answer to-night "It is true ! It is true '
At the breast of the Old we have nourished the New !
From the East and the West and the North we have come
To be rid of the wreck and the ruin of ruin ;
Where the Emory sings on its way to the sea
We have come from its curses our children to free ;
By the hope of our hearts, and the help of our hands,
In its beauty and strength Happy Harriman stands,
A surprise, a delight, in the fairest of lands ! "

GENERAL CLINTON B. FISK.

HARRIMAN.

ITS HISTORY AND TOPOGRAPHY.

PIONEERS' DAY, February 26, 1892,—the Second Anniversary of Harriman! A fit occasion, indeed, for putting to press this pamphlet which tells, with all the exactness of photography, what things have been done, in the short space of two years, where before that were only the cornfields and timber of an old plantation.

Twenty-four months of active effort,—less than that, to be precise, so far as permanent building at Harriman has gone. When the Great Sale occurred, which publicly inaugurated the town, building conditions were temporary, on the flat land near that old farm-house of Col. R. K. Byrd which formed the nucleus. Scores of "shacks" went up there like magic, in the rain and mud, just before the sale opened, and scores more followed through the spring and summer succeeding, until "Shacktown" numbered over a thousand souls. Then in September it was abandoned for the higher ground near by, where snug homes and more costly business blocks had been taking shape, though these did not actively progress, to any considerable extent, until two or three months after the sale.

7

WALL STREET IN "SHACKTOWN," SUMMER OF 1890.

The three days of that sale will be forever memorable among Harriman pioneers, and on the records of lot selling wherever kept. Less than 600 lots for over $600,000—who would believe it? Three thousand men, from fifteen States, wild to get lots at any price, hundreds of them having waited their chance for days, in mud and rain and misery, —who would credit such eagerness? What caused it? By what persuasive art had they been allured from the established cities and towns of Tennessee, Kentucky, Ohio, and a dozen other States, and imbued with a sublime faith in their fellows, in the new town site where lots were offered, in the city that here should rise?

ITS LOCATION.

At Big Emory Gap, in Roane County, Tennessee, where the Emory river breaks its way through Walden's Ridge, after its rapid descent from the Cumberland Plateau, it was ordained by nature that a town should be. Col. Byrd, who here held large ownership of land, always thus insisted, and died firm in such faith. Here, with coal close at hand on the west and on the north, and with iron near by on the east and within ten miles to the south, there was every essential condition for the establishment of a city with the purest water supply, the best natural drainage, picturesque surroundings, admirable climate. And here the East Tennessee Land Company located Harriman, within a crescent formed by the Emory river, between the Cincinnati Southern Railway on the west and the Walden's Ridge division of the East Tennessee, Virginia and Georgia Railway on the north; fifty miles west of Knoxville, via this latter line, eighty miles north of Chattanooga, and 233 miles south of Cincinnati, via the Cincinnati Southern Railway.

In this favored spot, in a State largely defended from saloon influences by the Four-mile Law, certain well-known

9

HARRIMAN JUNCTION, LOOKING EAST FROM EMORY GAP.

advocates of Prohibition had resolved on
dustrial town, where labor should have
homes and churches and schools might fi
chance, free from the liquor traffic. Chief a
determined on combining a great moral
principle with an extensive commercial e
clear demonstration and for the best indus
General Clinton B. Fisk, who had been the
didate for President in 1888, and whose mi
Tennessee, as Freedmen's Commissioner in
entire State at the close of the war, had giv
hold upon its people, and a high opinion o
and its future.

ITS NO-SALOON BASIS.

With his colleagues General Fisk agreed
essee offered favorable conditions for town
sort in which they believed; that from all t
they had acquired within it the liquor t
banned forever, by provision of title deed;
they should establish must become an o
thrift, sobriety, superior intelligence, and
character. In the Company's by-laws, a
Section 1 of Article IX declared:

Every contract, deed or other conveyanc
estate by the Company, shall contain a pro
the use of the property, or any building
purpose of making, storing or selling intoxi
as such.

Besides its enormous purchases of coal
lands upon the Cumberland Plateau and o
down the Tennessee river, the East Tenne
pany had secured over 12,000 acres of la
lands at and east of Emory Gap, and a por
site afforded by these, staked out on Chris

11

was surveyed and mapped in February, 1890. Some street improvements were begun, a few rough board buildings were put up, and on the 26th day of that month, in that year, Harriman was formally inaugurated by a public auction sale of lots, which continued a portion of two days thereafter.

ITS OPENING SALE.

The weather had been execrable, for it was "the rainy season," with more storms than customary; the accommodations were worse; but the crowd came, nothing could dampen its ardor, and 574 lots were sold for $604,000. The Company did not seek any such "boom," and sturdily opposed it, both before and after the bidding began. The auctioneer was literally compelled by the Company's management to knock down lots to the lowest bidder in many cases. But faith in the Company's character, and confidence in the location of the town, created enthusiasm unmatched at any public sale till this, and indicative of the surprising growth which was to follow. At the request of a committee of buyers, before the sale opened, the Company waived all building and other conditions, and consequently withdrew all specific pledges. "We are going to build Harriman," said Gen. Fisk, the Company's President. He was giving his best thought and effort to this end, when in the July following he died.

On the 7th of February, 1891, Harriman was incorporated as a city, by special enactment of the State Legislature, approved by the Governor March 6th, ensuing. Having adopted their special charter, by an almost unanimous popular vote, on the 2d of June thereafter the City Government was chosen by the citizens at a special election where 736 votes were cast, twelve of them by ladies, asserting their right of suffrage under a general State law,

12

which everybody outside of Harriman had forgotten, and because of a special condition which the charter contains.

The census of 1890 credited Harriman with 710 population. In December, 1891, the first city directory was compiled, and its compiler took a house-to-house enumeration which showed 3,672 residents, not counting the miners' families opposite. At this date the residents number not less than 4,000.

ITS APPEARANCE FROM POINTS AROUND.

It is impossible on this page to show the city site as it appeared two years ago. The negative of the only photograph then taken of it has been destroyed; and the engraving reproduced from the negative, with other valuable illustrations referring to Harriman's first year, went to ruin in the Park Place disaster at New York last fall. It was a good view of the town site, as the pamphlet "One Year of Harriman" attested, showing a part of the great bend in the Emory River sweeping half way around it, and outlining as a background the picturesque Emory Heights beyond. It was a view from Wahlen's Ridge below Emory Gap, and above the Byrd coal mine; a view from the same direction (west), and from the same point, as that which follows, but from a higher uplift, and with the camera set for a wider field. In the picture now shown there are preserved a few long "shacks" in the center foreground, near which, on their right, stands the Byrd mansion, utilized as the office of the East Tennessee Land Company the first six months,—a square, respectable plantation house of the old regime, occupied forty years by Col. Byrd; from which he was buried in 1885, and where his widow remained until the East Tennessee Land Company purchased her lands, then removing to Kingston, from which place she has never returned to behold the transformation.

BIRD'S-EYE VIEW OF HARRIMAN, FROM WALDEN'S RIDGE ON THE WEST.

Half a mile to the left, as you look at the Byrd mansion in the engraving now spoken of, and out of the range of view, stands an apology for another farm-house, or the relic of another —the old Margrave place. It is reputed to be more than eighty years old. It was the first residence of which we have knowledge on the site of Harriman —a log house originally, as one end of the structure shows, with one portion of it more pretentious at some later time, and

THE OLD BYRD MANSION.

between its two parts a huge chimney, before whose fire-place of uncommon breadth local tradition says that Gen. Jackson sat many times when journeying with his coach-and-four from the Hermitage to Washington. Within its walls a Governor was born, tradition further says; and at

THE OLD MARGRAVE HOUSE.

the birth of Harriman, as more authentic statements agree, fifteen men found sleep and shelter in its low attic chamber alone, through the nights of the great sale. Our engraving faithfully portrays its forlorn state of age and disrepair. It now awaits inevitable dissolution, on Margrave street—one of the finest avenues Harriman can boast—hidden, except on near approach, by several of the best houses thus far built, conspicuous among them being the handsome old-colonial residence of Mr. Walter C. Harriman. So long as the Margrave relic is preserved, the old and the new, on Margrave street, are in striking contrast.

From a point on the lower slope of Walden's Ridge, northeast of Emory Gap, and back of the old Margrave

RESIDENCE OF WALTER C. HARRIMAN, MARGRAVE STREET.

place, was obtained the view reproduced on the following page. From it a fair impression is derived of one side of the town only, for four distinct views are necessary to give a correct idea of the whole. This view is looking almost due southeast, and clearly traces Queen and Walden streets, which, like Crescent, Virginia, Georgia and Tennessee streets, on the east, or left, and Morgan and Carter on the right, make directly toward the river, this side the heights that bound the near horizon. Before they reach the Emory, the streets up which you look surmount a ridge that lifts longitudinally across the town, as to its original platted portion, rising to a height of perhaps r feet above the river banks, and sweeping gracefully down on either hand.

SOME CONSPICUOUS FEATURES BEHELD.

Crowning this uplift, along the crest of which runs Cumberland street, at right angles with Queen and Walden streets up which you have been looking, is the beautiful

BIRD'S-EYE VIEW OF HARRIMAN, FROM WALDEN'S RIDGE ON THE NORTH.

GRACE UNIVERSALIST CHURCH ON CUMBERLAND STREET.

THE CENTRAL SCHOOL BUILDING.

Fisk Park, heavily timbered, as was the entire ridge before these streets ran through. Facing it, on Cumberland, stands the Universalist Church, now nearing completion, and thus far the most costly and elegant church edifice erected—thanks to the liberality of Ferdinand Schumacher (whose great oatmeal mills at Akron, O., have given fortune to himself and good health to his patrons) and the active effort of young people's societies in the Universalist denomination throughout many States. As completed, it is to be a unique specimen of temple architecture, with combination front of brick and wood; large cathedral windows of stained glass, in rich designs; all the interior comforts of a church home, and commanding from its low tower a prospect of remarkable beauty and breadth. This tower will be a favorite outlook of visitors who lack time for a ride on to Walden's Ridge, up which, from Margrave street, a winding carriage drive is nearly finished, and along which the views are magnificent beyond words, with happy Harriman always at your feet.

After the church mentioned, the most conspicuous building upon the ridge which it crowns is the Central School, erected and furnished by the Land Company at a cost of $6,000, and opened with a full corps of teachers, under a carefully graded system, in September, 1892. This school, and an outlying auxiliary to it, were maintained by the Land Company at its own expense throughout the first school year; and as the city can have no funds available from taxation, for school purposes, until next fall, the Company is generously defraying the entire cost of the school system throughout this second school year also, there being eleven teachers employed, with Prof. W. D. McFarland as Principal.

To complete one's observation of Harriman, from the com-

manding eminences round about, and to form an accurate
idea of its topography and environment, one should cross
the Emory, and view the town site from the south, looking

toward Walden's
Ridge upon the west
and north. Crossing
is made by either of
two ferries, the one
at the Rolling Mill,
or the Byrd Ferry, a

APPROACH TO THE BYRD
FERRY.

mile above. The
town side approach
to the latter is near
the Byrd mansion,
and in the summer is

a romantic spot, canopied by overhanging boughs which
bend across the roadway, and partially walled in by the ex-
posed roots of gnarled and rugged trees. An artist here would
revel in the effects of water and wood, of light and shade

and color which abound, and which range the whole kaleidoscopic variety of the seasons. Our engraving hints of these and of the floral beauties and woodland pleasures which may be found along Emory Heights when spring appears.

ACROSS THE RIVER.

A massive pile of rock uprears itself close to the river brink about midway of the wide crescent which the heights describe, and offers lofty outlook. It is easily reached on horseback, and from its dome a fascinating panorama is presented of the rolling city site, of its hundreds of tasteful homes, of the green river's current below, and of the encircling ridge opposite, which holds the valley in like an arm, where the elbow gone. Where was the elbow once, the Gap now is a picturesque break in a beautiful mountain chain. Looking down stream to the right, one sees the Rolling Mills, smaller in appearance than would be supposed, because so far below, and catches glimpses through their clouds of smoke of Walnut Hills addition farther on in the same direct line. Turning to the left, one's upward sweep of vision takes in a part of the town's manufacturing portion, with its Belt Line Railway and Emory street, which parallel the river, and lingers finally upon the distant ridge, south of the Gap, where sky and mountains meet.

EXTENT OF THE TOWN SITE.

The first platted portion of Harriman contained about 11 acres, not counting in a wide area next the river, reserved for railway, factory and other purposes, lying entirely with the river's upper bend. In May, 189 , an addition was platted one mile east, for the special accommodation of workingmen who could not afford such prices as had been for a time established by the auction sale, and one hundred cottage houses were there built and occupied that year. It is known

PART OF THE MANUFACTURING PORTION, FROM EMORY HEIGHTS.

LOOKING NORTHWARD, FROM EMORY HEIGHTS.

as Walnut Hills Addition, and forms a thriving suburb of the city proper, of which it is a corporate part. It has a school and a church, and numbers over 600 population. Oak View Addition joins it, nearer the ridge, where colored residents have grouped themselves, with their own churches and schools ; and approaching this, from the west, comes Ridge View Addition, platted last fall, along the lower slopes of Walden's Ridge for nearly a mile beginning at the Gap, upon which are many of the finest villa sites the whole town affords.

Fisk Addition, now being platted by the Land Company as this pamphlet goes to press, lies within the lower bend of the Emory, or what is called the second Oxbow, and below Walnut Hills. It is even more beautiful for situation than the part of Harriman first platted, and it will soon have, no doubt, all the facilities which there in so short a time have been established. The Belt Line Railway is being extended to it, and some of the best new industries, including the blast furnace and a large furniture factory, will be located there. From various parts of it the views are magnificent in all directions, but particularly up Little Emory Gap to the Little Brushy and the Big Brushy mountains, lifting their summits royally far beyond.

Long before Harriman has the 50,000 people which are anticipated, these two portions of the town will have grown together, with a blast furnace and other intermediate industries linking them like the ligature of the Siamese Twins. The two oxbows of the Emory are twins indeed, and the several thousand acres of level and rolling lands which they comprise will furnish room for a half million inhabitants without crowding. And along their water frontage, beside the Belt Line also, can industries enough be planted to support them all. Thus far the portions of Harriman actually platted do not exceed 1,600 acres.

26

SCENERY NEAR HARRIMAN, UP CLIFTY CREEK

In due time the central thoroughfare of Harriman will be Roane street, a view down which is herewith shown. Roane street, until near Walnut Hills Addition, then Roane avenue on to Fisk Addition. This thoroughfare, commencing at the western edge of town, will approximate three miles in length; and with Emory street winding around on

WALNUT HILLS ADDITION—FROM THE WEST.

the south, and Margrave and Sevier streets sweeping partially around upon the north, it will furnish a splendid drive, surpassed only by that magnificent boulevard soon to line the crest of Walden's Ridge, or the park-like roadways that will one day wind along Emory Heights. The extension of Roane avenue is now being made past Walnut Hills.

LOOKING DOWN ROANE STREET.

A. W. WAGNALLS.

ITS HOMES AND HELPS.

CHARACTER AND RESIDENCES.

From its really permanent beginning, the homes of Harriman have been characterized by unusual comfort, good taste and evident fixity of home life. They betoken a community of superior refinement and of abiding quality. They show that their builders came here to live and not merely to stay awhile. Every visitor comments upon their evidence of a peculiar *home-building* spirit, which guarantees the future. It has been said that there are more residences in Harriman costing from $3,000 to $15,000 each than any other town of its age and size has ever shown. It is impossible for us to portray even one in ten of the houses that have been erected which are uncommon for their architectural beauty, as well as their cost, in cities of small size, and which have never been matched, perhaps, in any town only two years old. Several of the early residences were illustrated in our first anniversary pamphlet, and cannot be reproduced here.

The old-colonial style house of Mr. Walter C. Harriman (in memory of whose father, General Walter Harriman, the town was named) has been shown on a former page. One of the accompanying interior views will show the fire-place in the hall of it, which might well be contrasted with the fire-place in the old Margrave house near by. Other handsome houses are nearing completion on the same street, and mark that portion of the town as a favorite place of resi-

HALLWAY, RESIDENCE OF W. C. HARRIMAN.

dence. One year ago Margrave street existed only on paper. In one year more it will be a delightful avenue of charming homes.

Cumberland street, as has been stated, traverses the crest

LOOKING UP CUMBERLAND STREET.

FREDERICK GATES.

RESIDENCE OF FREDERICK GATES CUMBERLAND STREET.

HALLWAY, RESIDENCE OF FREDERICK GATES.

of the high ridge which runs across the town, and upon this street are many residences of an excellent class, a row of which are shown on the opposite page. At the eastern end of this street where the ridge slopes down somewhat abruptly toward the river, and where the street itself inersects Emory street, which half encircles the town, stands the elegant home of Mr. Frederick Gates, in whose brain Harriman was conceived. Mr. Gates is the Second Vice-President of the East Tennessee Land Company, and the President of the Cumberland Plateau Improvement Company, recently organized as auxiliary thereto, and his home commands a splendid prospect of the city, or large portions of it, which he and his colleagues have established. Its location was known in the early days of Harriman as "Cornstalk Heights." From the broad verandas of the house a good view of the winding river is had; of Walnut Hills, the pretty suburb on the northeast; and of Walden's Ridge and Emory Gap on the north and west. The hall of

INTERIORS, RESIDENCE OF W. B. WINSLOW.

PARLOR, IN RESIDENCE OF W. B. WINSLOW.

RESIDENCE OF S. K. PAIGE.

this residence is one of its most noticeable features within.

Upon the same street, only two blocks away, is the home of Mr. W. B. Winslow, of the well-known firm of Winslow & Anderson, the externals of which, as in so many cases of which Harriman can boast, indicate a refinement of taste, and a permanence of location, very marked indeed. Inside this residence such refinement further asserts itself, and in the elegant furnishing and in the general appearance of

RESIDENCE OF JUDGE C. W. NOTTINGHAM.

culture and comfort happily combined, so admirably shown in the exquisite engravings we give. Still another Cumberland street home, not yet quite finished, and awaiting occupancy, is the residence of Mr. S. K. Paige, President of the Paige Manufacturing Company, which vies with that of Mr. Gates, at the opposite end of the street, in costliness and architectural design. From this, as from all the residence sites in that part of town, a magnificent view of Emory Gap

RESIDENCE OF DAVID GIBSON, WALDEN STREET.

is had, with much of the town spread out below you, upon the lower slopes.

The residence of Mr. W. H. Russell, General Manager of the East Tennessee Land Company, is on this street, and is one of the block of houses shown on a former page. This was, perhaps, the first house erected on the street. Of its hospitality many visitors to Harriman can attest.

The home of C. W. Nottingham, Esq., City Judge, is on Clinton street, which for a large part of its length is now well built up in tasteful fashion, its houses showing a wide degree of variety in style, and all commanding a fine outlook.

Mr. David Gibson, of the Gibson Agricultural Works, is just completing a house on Walden Street, with unique front, and of general design very pleasing.

TYPICAL COTTAGES OF ARTISANS.

Even the homes of the cheapest class, such as abound in the manufacturing district, upon Clitty, Sewanee, Carter, Emory, and other streets, are noteworthy for their neatness,

41

and their general average as above homes of a similar class in other manufacturing places. We give an illustration of two houses typical of the rest, though hundreds are superior to these in size and cost.

LEADING TRIBUTARY CORPORATIONS.

The helps of Harriman are numerous and worthy of special attention. Fitly classed with these, and from a material standpoint ranking at the head, is the East Tenn-

THE DENNY AND BURR BLOCK, CORNER ROANE AND CRESCENT STREET.

essee Land Company, which inaugurated the town. It was organized in June, 1889, by General Clinton B. Fisk and a number of other gentlemen of wide reputation, either as reformers or in the business world. Its plans for Harriman were very broad, and its achievements have been very great. It is perhaps the only company engaged in a great South-

OFFICE BUILDING OF THE EAST TENNESSEE LAND COMPANY

EXPOSITION BUILDING.

then issued bonds in place of selling the third million to that amount. Its President is A. W. Wagnalls, of the well-known publishing firm of Funk & Wagnalls, New York City.

Subsidiary to the East Tennessee Land Company, as a permanent help to Harriman, is the East Tennessee Mining

AT THE STEAMBOAT LANDING.

SMITH & LAKE BLOCK, CORNER ROANE AND CRESCENT.

Company, organized in September, 1891, to which were leased all the coal and iron properties of the Land Company in the neighborhood of Harriman, and by which will its raw material, in coal, coke and iron ore, be supplied. Its authorized capital stock is $1,000,000. It is operating the Tennessee River Iron Mines, about ten miles from Harriman, of which there are three, yielding a monthly output of several thousand tons; a mine just opened within the

W. H. RUSSELL

city's limits, from which ore is supplied to the Lookout Rolling Mills; and the Byrd Coal Mine, and the coke ovens in connection therewith, from which Harriman has drawn most of her fuel up to this time. A second coal mine has been just opened on the town side of the river in Walden's Ridge, which will double the coal supply.

The office building of the East Tennessee Land Company is a substantial brick and stone structure, erected upon a square reserved for public buildings, and bounded by Roane, Walden, Morgan and Trenton streets. The four Norman towers of the office building give it a peculiar appearance of grace and strength combined. It is pronounced the finest building of any kind in Roane county, and the finest private office building in the state. It was erected at a cost of about \$26,000, being completed in August, 1891. In this building are grouped the various offices of the Land Company, its three stories being fully occupied, and affording none too much room. Its interior finish throughout is with the native oak of the locality, and very elegant. It has a large fireproof vault, with all the attachments of a bank vault, and its appointments in every way are first-class.

The Belt Line Railway, which was built and is operated by the Harriman Coal and Iron Railroad Company affords a special feature of advantage for manufacturers as also for the general public. This line of road, deflecting from the East Tennessee, Virginia & Georgia Railway, a half mile from the junction of that road with the Cincinnati Southern Railway, extends nearly around the first platted portion of the town, and when the circuit is completed that section of it will be about four miles in extent. Its neat station is photographed on another page. It is a thoroughly substantial piece of railroad, and it is now being extended down to the second oxbow of the Emory, so as to encircle

48

ROANE STREET STATION, BELT LINE RAILWAY.

and accommodate the new Fisk Addition being platted there. This road makes it possible for all the industrial plants of Harriman to be located on a line of railway, and also to have water frontage if they so desire.

Reliable banking institutions are a vital necessity to the upbuilding of an industrial town. Harriman has three such, established in the following order : The First National Bank, capital $50,000 ; the Manufacturers' National Bank, capital $50,000 ; and the Harriman Bank and Trust Company, capital $25,000. The latter, of which Mr. James McDowell is President, has a savings department. Mr. J. D. Wolstenholme, President of the Manufacturers' National Bank, is also Secretary and Manager of the Harriman Building and Loan Association, W. H. Russell, President, which has been as helpful to Harriman as another bank would be. It has an authorized capital of $1,000,000, with $750,000 subscribed, and its loans for building purposes in Harriman are very large. The Harriman Improvement Company, Mr. L. S. Freeman, President, has been also an efficient help ; original capital, $75,000 ; increase to $150,000 just authorized.

The Harriman *Advance* has done much to advertise and aid the city, whose career is tersely summed up in that paper's name. It began with daily issues only, but is now published in both daily and weekly editions by the Advance Printing Company, Gideon Hill, President. A. A. Hopkins is its Editor-in-Chief ; W. S. Hallock, Managing Editor ; J. W. Bridwell, City Editor. The Harriman *Weekly Times* has been lately established.

Various minor building and other companies have aided in Harriman's growth. The Fales Building Company has erected the finest private business block thus far built, on Walden street. The Bank Building Company has been incorporated, for the erection, corner of Roane and Walden

HARRIMAN BANK AND TRUST COMPANY.

streets, of a still finer block, to accommodate the Manufacturers' Bank, the Building and Loan Association, and the Daily and Weekly *Advance*.

The Harriman Manufacturing Company has been, and will remain, the chief promoter of industries at Harriman. It was chartered under the statutes of Tennessee, with broad powers and privileges, on the 16th day of October, 1890, to be the right arm of the East Tennessee Land Company in its great work. Its organization was perfected on the 20th of November ensuing, with the following list of officers :

President — JOHN HOPEWELL, Jr.

Treasurer — A. W. WAGNALLS.

Secretary — A. A. HOPKINS.

General Manager — W. H. RUSSELL.

Its capital stock was fixed at $1,000,000—thereby adding potentially this amount to the moderate capitalization of the Land Company, and still further assuring the necessary funds for development—and over $300,000 of it were subscribed before its active operations began.

The plans and methods of this Manufacturing Company were novel in their character, and were devised and perfected after careful deliberation by the directors and managers of the East Tennessee Land Company, in consultation with prominent business men not previously connected with the Land Company's affairs.

CHRISTIAN HELPS.

The churches of Harriman should be mentioned first among its moral and beneficent helps. There are nine different church organizations which have regular worship, and of these the Congregational, the First Methodist, the Southern Methodist, the Christian, and two colored churches, meet regularly in their own houses, but only the Christian Church yet occupies its permanent church edifice, an illus-

52

tration of which appears. The others have erected neat chapels, the Congregationalists leading the way, with Fisk Chapel soon after dedicated by the First Methodist organization. Each of these, as also the Southern Methodist, will, in due time, erect their main edifice upon the front of the lots donated by the East Tennessee Land Company.

Reference has been made to the Universalist church, now nearly finished. The Baptists, the Universalists, the Episco-

THE CHRISTIAN CHURCH, MORGAN STREET.

palians, and the Presbyterians, have service regularly in temporary quarters, the former occupying the Y. M. C. A. hall. The Baptists, however, have begun their permanent house of worship on Trenton, corner of Queen street, which will be a substantial brick edifice, erected near the business center of town. The Episcopalians have also begun the erection of a church on Trenton street. The dwellers in Harriman are a church-going people, to a degree unusual even in the most moral communities. Each of the church organizations has a resident minister.

The Young Men's Christian Association was organized over a year ago, and has been zealously conducted ever since. It has rooms in the Caldwell block, one of the best business buildings thus far erected, where is a comfortable hall seating about 400, and where it has a considerable library. It meditates the erection of a suitable building of its own. The State Y. M. C. A. honored it by holding its annual session in Harriman last September.

The Women's Christian Temperance Union was early organized, and has been a very active helper in the development of temperance zeal, and in the support of the policy inaugurated by the East Tennessee Land Company. The latter liberally donated lots to the Union for the erection of a Temple, which was sufficiently completed in September last to allow the holding in it of the State W. C. T. U. convention, which gathered there. The Temple, as appears from our engraving, is a very creditable piece of architecture, its total cost being about $8,000. The money for its erection has been cheerfully donated by townspeople and outside friends, with the exception of a certain amount of indebtedness soon to be liquidated. The seating capacity of the Temple is about one thousand, and it has small rooms for meetings of the Union, parlor accommodations, etc. It affords the best and largest place for public gatherings thus far provided.

HOTEL ACCOMMODATIONS.

Harriman has several hotels and boarding houses of an excellent character, chief of which is the Hotel Cumberland, on Devonia street, within two blocks of the stopping place

W. C. T. U. TEMPLE.

for all trains on the E. T. V. & G. R. R.   This hotel, begun
by private parties, was finished with funds provided by the
E. T. L. Company, into whose hands passed a controlling interest in the stock of the Hotel Company one year ago.   It
will accommodate from one hundred to one hundred and
fifty guests, is provided with steam heat, baths and all sani-
tary features, affords the best table in the entire region, and
has become popular with commercial men and tourists on

CUMBERLAND HOTEL.

this account.   It commands a superb view of Emory Gap
and Walden's Ridge, which it faces.   The summer nights
here are deliciously cool and agreeable, because of the cool
breeze which makes out of the Gap regularly in the after-
noon and evening of every summer day.

Within one block of it is the extensive foundation of the
great hotel originally planned by the Land Company, when
it did not appear that private enterprise would build a public house equal to the character and requirements of the

FALES BLOCK.

RESIDENCE OF W. H. RUSSELL. CUMBERLAND STREET.

place, the erection of which was suspended when the Company found it necessary to assume such large share in the ownership of the Cumberland. In due time, when the demands of the town make necessary, its completion will no doubt be carried forward, and it will become a conspicuous landmark of Harriman, as beheld by all who pass on either of the railroads.

ON THE EMORY AT HARRIMAN.

JOHN HOPEWELL, JR.

ITS INDUSTRIES

Industrially, the two years of Harriman furnish a record that differentiates it from all other new towns of the South. Its builders did not make the early mistake, so common, of assuming that a blast furnace is the *sine qua non* of success in town building, and that upon a furnace alone can a town be successfully established. They counted on seeing the furnace a fact in due time, where all conditions favor its profitable operation, but they believed its establishment might fitly wait until other industries should create local demand for its product, and thereby assure its profit. They were certain that a variety of manufacture would best guarantee the industrial success desired ; and that it was wiser to locate several small concerns, on sound business principles, with an output soon to follow, and with fair assurances of growth, than to seek two or three extensive plants, requiring heavy bonus, which might be a year in course of erection, and the products of which must be long delayed.

Results have justified this policy, as in Harriman alone has steady progress been made in the development of Southern industries. This fact is due, in about equal measure, to the methods that were adopted for such development there, and to the superior opportunities and advantages which Harriman affords. These methods excluded the bonus idea from the first, and were based on genuine reciprocation; these advantages made that reciprocation sufficient, and bonuses less requisite. In other words, it has been found that certain reciprocal features peculiar to Harriman, and a combination of resources not elsewhere existing in such

HARRIMAN'S FIRST INDUSTRY—OLD SAW MILL.

favorable degree, furnish ample reason for manufacturers to locate there.

Briefly stated, the Harriman Manufacturing Company's plan was and is to invest its capital in manufacturing industries at Harriman, to the extent of from one-third to one-half the capital necessary to establish an industry, outside capital being interested to the extent of one-half to two-thirds in each case.

THE LOOKOUT ROLLING MILLS.

The Manufacturing Company will thus hold a large interest, as it does already, in many substantial factories at Harriman, and through proper officers will exercise careful supervision over these, making sure they are conducted to the best possible advantage, and that all means within the power of the Harriman Manufacturing Company and of the

A GLIMPSE IN THE ROLLING MILLS.

East Tennessee Land Company are used to promote their welfare and assure a wide market for their products.

CO-OPERATIVE METHODS.

This plan, it is believed, will carry to the utmost point yet attained, the spirit and method of co-operation among manufacturing establishments of different character, so that all shall work as one concern for their own interest, the interest of the town, and the consequent greater success of the parent company. Under it each industry which locates at Harriman may hope to make greater profits upon its capital

AN INTERIOR VIEW OF LOOKOUT ROLLING MILL.

than could be made by the same investment, as an independent enterprise, at any other place in the South. There are possibilities of mutual gain, for many industries working in harmonious combination, which cannot separately be commanded, and the co-operative advantages which may be secured by the Harriman Manufacturing Company, for manufactures at Harriman, and for the profitable handling

PUDDLING FURNACES, LOOKOUT ROLLING MILL.

and sale, away from Harriman, of whatever may be there produced, will readily suggest themselves. They make it feasible for one man, or one set of men, in many market centers, to care for the interests of several related industries, at great saving of expense, and great increase of profit to each. It follows that the stock to be held in each, by the Harriman Manufacturing Company, must be a profitable source of income to that Company, and must make its own stock return handsome dividends and increase handsomely

GIBSON AGRICULTURAL WORKS.

FITST SHIPMENT OF PLOWS, GIBSON AGRICULTURAL WORKS.

in value. This is the more certain because the stock which the Harriman Company will hold in many subordinate companies will be preferred stock, with six per cent. dividend fairly assured upon it, by such preference, from the start.

In consideration of the industries to be located at Harriman, and of advantages to accrue from their location there under the plan above set forth, the East Tennessee Land

FORGE ROOMS, AGRICULTURAL WORKS.

Company entered into a contract with the Harriman Manufacturing Company whereby the former company is to make over, in March and September of each year, an amount of money sufficient, with any moneys in the treasury of the Harriman Manufacturing Company applicable to the payment of dividends, to insure a semi-annual dividend of three per cent. upon all stock of the Harriman Manufacturing Company outstanding. Under this agreement, which assured three per cent. semi-annual dividend to all the stock of the Harriman Manufacturing Company for the term of four years, two such dividends have already been paid.

The methods of the Harriman Manufacturing Company are conservative and practical, though peculiar to itself. It avoids the bonus system in the location of industries, and seeks their establishment at Harriman only upon plain business principles. It engages to secure from the East Tennessee Land Company, in pursuance of the contract with that

SAW AND BENDING DEPARTMENT, GIBSON AGRICULTURAL WORKS.

Company, to which reference has already been made, a suitable site for each manufacturing concern established at Harriman, the same being donated by the East Tennessee Land Company under that contract; and the Harriman Manufacturing Company then insists that for every dollar which it shall invest in a manufacturing concern, the men who are actively to become its managers, for themselves or others, shall invest a like amount, either in cash, or its

HARRIMAN HOE AND TOOL FACTORY.

equivalent' in machinery or material. Under this arrangement the Harriman Manufacturing Company comes into ownership, without cost, of valuable real estate franchises, and the cash invested by it represents actual values without inflation or bonuses for good-will. Moreover, the men who actively manage those concerns thus located at Harriman have at least equal interest in their economical and energetic administration, and their success.

Careful selection of industries is made, with a view to such relation thereof as shall render them patrons of each other, as much as possible, thus insuring for each, to the largest possible extent, a local supply of raw material without transportation charges, and with a large home market for the article produced. Under this plan and by these methods this Manufacturing Company has advantages peculiar to itself, and enjoyed by no other company known, viz :

PECULIAR ADVANTAGES.

1st.—It groups the best possibilities of several kinds of manufacture, under advantageous conditions nowhere else to be found.

2d.—It gives to the investor a guarantee of profit, from such varied manufacture, not possible from one line of industry alone.

3d.—It backs this guarantee by a responsible contract, making doubly sure the semi-annual payment of a good dividend for a term of years.

Up to the 1st of November, 1891, this Company had located at Harriman, under this plan and by these methods, the following nine industries :

INDUSTRIES IN OPERATION.

Lookout Rolling Mills.—Lookout Iron Company, capital $2,0,0,0 ; removed from Chattanooga ; Sol. Simpson, president : J. D. Roberts, manager : 200 hands employed before removal ; mills largely increased in size : 250 to 300 hands.

Gibson Agricultural Works. — Gibson Agricultural

72

FORGE DEPARTMENT, HOE AND TOOL FACTORY.

Works Company, capital $5,000; David Gibson, president; removed from Chattanooga; 70 hands employed there; capacity doubled; 125 to 150 hands.

Harriman Hoe and Tool Factory. — Harriman Hoe and Tool Co., newly established; Louis B. Goodall, president; George B. Durell, manager; capital $75,000; 40 to 60 hands.

Harriman Tack Factory. — Harriman Tack Company, reorganized after removal from Auburn, N. Y.; capital $40,000; A. A. Hopkins, president; J. H. P. Lane, superintendent; 20 to 40 hands.

East Tennessee Furniture Factory. — East Tennessee Furniture Co., capital $25,000; removed from Knoxville; W. H. Russell, president; M. L. Dame, manager; 30 to 60 hands.

Duthie Machine Works and Foundry. — Duthie Machine and Foundry Co., capital $20,000; removed from Knoxville; George H. Duthie, president and manager; 40 hands.

Harriman Brick Works. — Harriman Brick and Building Company, new organization, capital $30,000; E. M. Goodall, president; 20 hands.

Cumberland Manufacturing Works. — (Building material, sash, blinds, etc.) Cumberland Manufacturing Co., new; capital $25,000; Frederick Gates, president; 30 hands.

Bailey Auger Works. — Bailey Auger Bit Co., capital $50,000; removed from Lancaster, O.; W. A. Starbuck, president; J. K. Hayward, secretary and treasurer; R. M. True, manager; 20 to 60 hands.

All these nine industries were in successful operation on the date named, with their production supplying local demands, or shipping their products to various points north,

THE HARRIMAN TACK FACTORY.

south, east and west. Nearly all were behind actual orders, and the Lookout Rolling Mills were turning out iron for shipment on orders direct to Louisville, Cincinnati and Pittsburgh, thus demonstrating that Harriman is far enough south to insure the cheapest iron-making conditions, and sufficiently farther north than Alabama to command the Northern markets, and to compete successfully with Pennsylvania iron makers for the best iron trade. Since that date the Rolling Mills have successfully rolled steel plates, for the Hoe and Tool Factory, from Southern steel billets, made at the Southern Steel Works in Chattanooga, thus demonstrating that the South has her own facilities for all forms of steel production, and that Harriman's own industries largely afford supplies for each other.

Up to the date last mentioned the stock held by the Harriman Manufacturing Company in the above industries aggregated $268,000, of which over $100,000 was preferred.

Upon the date which these pages commemorate—February 26, 1892, second anniversary of Harriman—a new announcement is made by the East Tennessee Land Company, which has vital significance to Harriman and her industrial future.

The Land Company agrees and guarantees that from and after this date one-half the net proceeds of all its lot sales at Harriman, and one-half the net proceeds of all Income Warrants sold after March 1st, and applied on lot payments, until such net proceeds reach the total amount of $2,000,000, shall be set apart as an Industrial Fund, for the establishment and promotion of industries at Harriman. By this agreement and guarantee the sum of *One Million Dollars*, as it may become available from sales made, is appropriated by the East Tennessee Land Company for the industrial growth of Harriman ; or, to put it more plainly still, one-

half the net sum received by the Company, from the sale of every lot, until the broad limit is reached as fixed above, is to be applied for the buyer's direct benefit, by manufacturing investment that shall increase the value of every lot sold.

Under the plan and by the methods of the parent Company, and its auxiliary, as heretofore set forth, every dollar industrially invested must be matched by at least another dollar of capital from an outside source; and this fact really means for every lot purchaser at Harriman, during the next year or two, an actual investment for manufactures there, as the direct result of his purchase, of *cash equivalent to the full sum he pays*: if total lot sales reach that amount, an aggregate investment for industries at Harriman, by and because of the Land Company's action, of *an even Two Millions of Dollars*. It is computed that such a sum thus applied would carry the population of Harriman, within its first five years, to not less than 25,000 souls. The establishment of an Industrial Fund so large, under conditions that must be so far-reaching, witnesses to great faith in Harriman's future, and astonishing liberality of purpose to insure the same.

The first fruits of the sagacious and liberal policy thus inaugurated for Harriman, are apparent even before these pages leave the press, in a large number of plants offered for location there, and in a contract actually made to remove the Hayes Chair Factory from Tallapoosa, Ga., and to operate its business by the Hayes Chair Company, of Harriman; capital, $75,000: capacity 50 to 75 hands.

Apart from any ownership of the Harriman Manufacturing Company there are several enterprises at Harriman now in operation or soon to be, of considerable extent and much credit to the town. Easily first of these is the S. K. Paige Manufacturing Works, with capacity for 150 hands; S. K. Paige Manufacturing Company, capital $50,000: Mr. S. K.

DUTHIE MACHINE AND FOUNDRY WORKS.

Paige, President; W. C. Harriman, Treasurer; W. V. Hawkes, Manager. This concern is for working altogether in wood; the making of wooden-ware; the production of finished wood-stuff in varied forms. It is a model factory with all recent appliances for utilizing power and skill.

The Emory River Ice Company, J. D. Wolstenholme, President, will manufacture ice this season from the pure water which the Emory supplies, and with a plant costing $20,000.

The Whipple & Armstrong Machine Works, beginning in a modest fashion, anticipate success and attendant growth.

CHEAP MANUFACTURING CONDITIONS.

No other town in the South can match the manufacturing conditions which Harriman affords for cheapness of production and ease of shipment. An ample supply of water so pure that even steam boilers are not encrusted by its use; water frontage when desired and river transportation a part of each year; a Belt Line Railway, reaching directly every manufacturing concern, with its own switches provided; trunk line freight facilities excellent and sure to increase; a climate neither so cold in winter nor so hot in summer as to interfere with advantageous indoor work:—these are some of the superior advantages offered. Then the timber resources round about Harriman are extensive; and the Harriman Coal and Iron Railroad, now extending into the Brushy Mountain region, twenty miles away, will develop extensive resources of coal, lumber, etc., all tributary to the manufacturing interests at Harriman, and easily to be commanded for their advantage. Moreover, the coal and iron mines of the East Tennessee Land Company are in close touch with the town, one coal mine being in active operation just across the river, another now being opened on the town side, and three iron mines, yielding their output of thousands of tons of ore each month, but ten to twelve miles away,

S. K. PAIGE MANUFACTURING WORKS.

and soon to be accessible by the river division of the Harriman Coal and Iron Railroad, the completion of which is expected within the coming year.

Immense iron deposits commence on the eastern edge of Harriman and extend several miles along the ridges which parallel the Cumberland plateau, running eastward towards Knoxville, fifty miles away. These iron deposits have been lately opened for supplying their hard ore to the Harriman Wrought Iron Furnace and to the Lookout Rolling Mills, and prove greatly superior to similar deposits farther south; and coal of the Byrd mine, at Harriman, is pronounced by users there far better than any which they had previously used for forge and rolling mill purposes.

Mr. D. A. Plant, superintendent of the Lookout Rolling Mills, being inquired of as to this coal, testified thus: "I consider the Byrd coal of a very good quality, free to burn, and carrying with it a clean and fierce combustion, a quality very necessary for the making and heating of iron. It also possesses good lasting qualities, which are so seldom found in a great many of the free burning coals such as Poplar Creek, Jellico and others. The coals used mainly in Chattanooga were from Daisy, Sale Creek and Soddy; these coals could not be used with any satisfaction at all without the aid of strong blast, thus causing continued repairing to furnaces to keep them in working order. These coals also make very heavy clinkers in the fire chambers, the result of which consumed a great deal of time in cleaning grates and getting furnaces sufficiently hot to charge next heat.

"The Byrd coal works just the reverse of the coal mentioned above. We can use it without blast, thus avoiding a great deal of the expense in repairing, caused by using blast. This coal does not clinker, but burns down to a fine ash; thus it requires little or no time to clean grates, leaving

THE HARRIMAN BRICK YARD.

CUMBERLAND MANUFACTURING WORKS.

the furnaces at all times hot enough to charge right along. Hence, there is no comparison between this and the coal used in Chattanooga ; and with this difference in our favor, I feel safe in saying that there must be a saving of from 20 to 25 per cent. in the coal item, compared with Chattanooga."

Coal of like quality abounds in Walden's Ridge for miles on the border of the city site, and extending eastward, while the Brushy Mountain coal fields, to be developed by the Brushy Mountain division of the Harriman Coal and Iron Railroad, are pronounced by experts of great richness and inexhaustible supply. Coke of good quality is already made by the East Tennessee Mining Company, at the Byrd mine, which finds use in the factories there, giving excellent satisfaction, while a still better quality is anticipated from the Brushy Mountain mines as soon as these shall be developed.

Mr. David Gibson, President of the Gibson Agricultural Works, under date of Nov. 25th, 1891, wrote thus about the coke made from this Byrd mine coal :

"I am very glad to report that I have never used better coke than I am getting from you. In the cupola it holds its burden well, burns freely and is very clean. I have used Connellsville and Pocahontas coke, and consider this equal to any I have ever used in the cupola, and *better* than either of the others in the forge, for the reason that it burns more freely, does not form into clinkers, and the ash drops away freely, so that we can keep a clean fire. It is especially good for welding on this account. Mr. Jerry Clark, superintendent of the Hoe and Tool Works just stepped in, and I asked his opinion of the coke, and his report exactly coincides with my ideas. He finds it the best he has ever used, and he is an expert hoe manufacturer and has spent all his life in this business, which requires the best of fuel."

THE BAILEY AUGER BIT WORKS.

SAVING TO MANUFACTURERS.

It has been and will be easy to locate desirable industries at Harriman without payment of bonuses usually exacted from new towns, because of the clear saving in manufacture, effected chiefly in three ways, viz:

1st.—By the proximity, cheapness and easy command of raw material, iron and timber.

2d.—By the low cost of coal for fuel, delivered at factory doors by the East Tennessee Mining Company for from $1.25 to $1.50 per ton.

3d.—By the river and railroad facilities enjoyed, all factories being located on the Belt Railroad, encircling Harriman, and also, if they wish it, beside the Emory river, parallel therewith.

As stated by Mr. Sol. Simpson, president of the Lookout Iron Company, the Lookout Rolling Mills, which before their removal had done a successful business at Chattanooga for several years, will save $12,000 a year in the cost of coal alone, or six per cent. on the entire capital, by locating at Harriman. They will save, also, nearly all their water rent, about $25 per month, taking their supply directly from the river, near which the great plant stands. They will also save greatly in the use of iron ore, and the total saving on their output, as compared with cost of an equal output at Chattanooga (had such an output been there possible), is computed by the superintendent at $25,000 a year. The Gibson Agricultural Works will also make a correspondingly large saving in the use of coals and hard woods.

An abundance of iron, coke and limestone, in the nearest contiguity known anywhere, makes it certain that Harriman will be able to produce iron as cheaply at least as it can anywhere be produced in the world. Says Dr. George A. Koenig, Professor of Metallurgy and Mining in the University of Pennsylvania:

"I do not hesitate to make the assertion that iron can be made here at a greater profit than at Birmingham."

Says Jo. C. Guild, Assistant State Geologist of Tennessee, and Mining Engineer :

"All the conditions are present for the cheap manufacture of iron—an abundance of iron ore, both hard and soft; an inexhaustible supply of good coking coal, and good limestone for flux on every hand; all these secured in a stone's throw of each other."

Says Capt. J. D. Roberts, Manager of the Lookout Rolling Mills :

"Harriman is second to none in her facilities for the manufacture of pig iron and basic steel at a low cost."

These things being true, and the manufactures already established at Harriman making a local demand for pig iron nearly or quite equal to the output of one furnace, the Harriman Furnace Company has been organized, Ferd. Schumacher, President; W. B. Winslow, Secretary, with an authorized capital of $500,000, of which one-half is common stock, and the other half an 8 per cent. Cumulative Preferred stock. All the Common Stock has been subscribed for by the East Tennessee Land Company and the East Tennessee Mining Company, the latter of which, desiring a local market for its products, contracts to furnish iron ore and coke to the extent of 250,000 tons of each per annum, at $2.50 per ton for coke, and $1.5 per ton for iron ore, these being the maximum figures. It will guarantee the coke to be equal in quality to any produced in the South ; that the iron ore shall make a 40 per cent mixture ; that its quality shall be second to none of the hematite ores now used in the South ; and that it will make, as it has proven by actual experience, the best grade of foundry pig, and Basic pig for any of the open

STREET SCENES IN HARRIMAN

hearth processes. Average analysis of the cokes and ore which will be furnished is as follows :

COKE.

	Per Cent.
Fixed carbon,	90
Ash,	8
Sulphur,	1
Moisture,	1

IRON ORE.

	Per Cent.
Metallic iron,	50
Alumina,	6
Silica,	10
Sulphur,	60
Phosphorus,	0.4
Moisture,	10
Total,	70.4

Limestone can be obtained within eighty rods of Furnace, containing :

	Per Cent
Carb. Lime from	75 to 95
Magnesia carb. from	3 to 22
Silica,	1 to 5

Taking these figures as a basis, pig iron can be produced with modern furnace plant, at Harriman, at a cost of $10 per ton as follows :

2.50 tons iron ore at $1.50	$3.75
1.50 " coke " " 2.50	3.75
limestone,	.50
Labor, salaries, incidentals and interest on plant and repairs,	2.00
Total,	$10.00
Labor, etc., on single 100-ton furnace, $2.50	
" " " pair " " 2.00	

All the mill irons to the extent of 70 tons per day, and some of the No. 2 foundry, can be sold here in Harriman to the Lookout Iron Co., the Agricultural Works and Foundries, at a profit of not less than $1.00 per ton on mill, and $2.00 on foundry grades, during the seasons of lowest prices which have yet prevailed, and $2.00 per ton on all foundry grades shipped to other points. Or, to average the whole output, every ton of iron made should yield a profit of not less than $1.25 per ton, based on present prices, which are the lowest in the history of the trade.

TIP HOUSE OF THE BYRD MINE, WITH COKE OVENS, AT HARRIMAN.

The *Cumulative Preferred Stock* is entitled to Eight Per Cent. of the Company's profits before the Common Stock receives any dividend, and will share with the Common Stock pro rata, after that receives Eight Per Cent. in all the profits in excess thereof. If the profits in any year do not equal Eight Per Cent. upon the Preferred Stock, the deficit in dividend remains a charge against the future profits, to be paid therefrom. The Preferred Stock also has a lien on the assets of the Company superior to that of the Common Stock, which entitles it to be paid in full before the principal of any

PROPOSED MODEL FURNACE, AT HARRIMAN.

part of the Common Stock shall be paid. These preferences make it absolutely secure as an investment.

Of the *Cumulative Preferred Stock* $50,000 has been subscribed for, by the Harriman Manufacturing Co., and the remaining $200,000 *is being taken by outside parties, at par.* Shares are $100 each.

LOOKING DOWN WALDEN STREET.

SOBRIETY OF LABOR.

Already the character of Harriman for sobriety and thrift is attracting wide-spread attention from manufacturers, and the moral aspect of the town, with the certainty of sober workingmen, because of the absence of saloons, will more and more induce the location of desirable manufacturing plants. It is a well-known economic fact that sober labor, away from saloons, yields a positive percentage of gain to the capital employing it, over labor in a community where the liquor traffic is allowed. Statistics could here be cited were it necessary, to show that this is the fact, and that large manufacturing plants have actually yielded a much larger interest upon their capital in years when the liquor traffic around them was forbidden and abolished, than in years when the liquor traffic was permitted, but with the same financial conditions otherwise. By the policy of the East Tennessee Land Company the liquor traffic is prohibited in title deeds, and saloons can never be permitted, with their inevitable influences upon labor and its product. It has already been demonstrated at Harriman that the best manufacturing conditions abound where sobriety exists. No class of workingmen ever is so profitable to its employers as the class which can come and does come, by reason of its labor, into the ownership of its own homes, covets permanency of employment, strives after superiority, and seeks that mutual welfare which labor and capital should each assure to each. Already the number of homes owned at Harriman by the workingmen employed there surpasses, as is believed, that of any other town of like population.

PROFITABLE INVESTMENT.

Because of sober labor, working at its best and producing the largest possible output upon the basis of capital employed; because of raw material close at hand, cheaply accessible, and easily commanded at the lowest possible cost ; and because of the co-operative features, insuring mutuality of effort, manufacture of every kind must be reduced at Harriman to the minimum of expense ; and under the practical business management secured for each concern, by the methods which have been outlined, the profits of the manufacturing plants at Harriman must be greater than elsewhere they can average ; and by reason of the contract and virtual guarantee already mentioned, it is certain that the stock of the Harriman Manufacturing Company will pay fair dividends during the first years when industries are becoming established. It is equally certain from the conditions referred to, that said stock will constantly grow in its dividend-paying capacity, and that all who invest in it will find their investment of steadily increasing value. There seems no reason why the Harriman Manufacturing Company shall not become one of the most extensive and most profitable of all the industrial enterprises which have taken root in the South, or which have been presented to the public for general subscription ; and the Management cordially invite the most scrutinizing examination of Harriman's industries, and of the methods of this Company, by all who seek investment.

Of the remainder of the $1,000,000 of stock untaken, $25 ,000 is now offered for sale at par. Shares are $50 each and where five or more shares are ordered at any one time, twenty per cent. payment may be made down, the balance being payable in monthly installments of like amount. It should be clearly understood that this stock, unlike the industrial stocks generally offered and liberally taken, is of *uniform value and advantage!*

A. A. HOPKINS.

OUR HARRIMAN.

(Air—"Watch on the Rhine.")

Lift up your voice in glad acclaim,
  O ye who gather here to-day,
And echo every heart the name
  To which we loving tribute pay.

O Harriman, dear Harriman !
  May peace be thine, forever thine !
Brave hearts, and true, in love thy ways defend,
  While heaven's blessings on thy homes descend.

Here field and forest waited long
  The music of the hammer's ring,
The thrill of Labor's cheerful song,
  And bounty that the years might bring.

O Harriman, dear Harriman !
  Thy mountains look with pride on thee ;
Hope, faith and courage here have builded well,
  Long may their faith and works thy people tell !

Here loyal hearts and willing hands
  Have lifted high their banners brave,
And heeding Love's divine commands
  Have sought the tempted soul to save.

O Harriman, glad Harriman !
  Thy banners wave till o'er the world
Manhood shall stand in faith for God and Right
  And Love shall rule the land with Love's own might.

O Harriman, young Harriman,
  Grow strong and bold through all the years,
As if within thy pulses ran
  The blood of thine own pioneers.

O Harriman, our Harriman !
  The skies above in blessings bend ;
Heav'n hear the prayer for thee that each heart lift
  And fill thy future with its choicest gifts.

97

East Tennessee Land Company.

HARRIMAN, TENN.

OFFICERS:

A. W. WAGNALLS, President.

JOHN HOPEWELL, Jr., First Vice-President.

FREDERICK GATES, Second Vice-President.

W. H. RUSSELL, General Manager.

A. A. HOPKINS, Secretary.

J. D. WOLSTENHOLME, Treasurer.

GEO. W. EASLEY, General Counsel.

DIRECTORS:

J. E. HOBBS,	JOHN HOPEWELL, Jr.
A. W. WAGNALLS	J. H. WHITMORE.
F. SCHUMACHER.	J. C. SNOW,
L. S. FREEMAN.	H. M. WINSLOW,
FREDERICK GATES.	WM. SILVERWOOD,
W. H. RUSSELL.	E. M. GOODALL.

A. A. HOPKINS.

oN

Harriman Manufacturing Company.

HARRIMAN, TENN.

OFFICERS:

JOHN HOPEWELL, Jr., President.

FERD. SCHUMACHER, Vice-President.

W. H. RUSSELL, General Manager.

J. D. WOLSTENHOLME, Treasurer.

A. A. HOPKINS, Secretary.

DIRECTORS:

John Hopewell, Jr.	Ferd. Schumacher.
Frederick Gates.	A. W. Wagnalls.
W. H. Russell.	A. A. Hopkins.
J. D. Rogers.	J. D. Wolstenholme.

J. H. Whittmore

THE HARRIMAN BUILDING AND LOAN ASSOCIATION.

CAPITAL, $1,000,000.

Operates as a Local Building Association or Co operative Bank.

Its funds are loaned on Improved Harriman Real Estate, no Loan exceeding 60 per cent. of the value of the security.

Loans are paid off in monthly installments, so that the risk of the Association is being constantly decreased.

The Association has declared three semi-annual dividends of 9 per cent. each, or at the rate of 18 per cent. per annum. There is every reason to believe that future earnings will be even more satis factory.

A limited amount of stock is still for sale.

Address for further particulars,

HARRIMAN BUILDING AND LOAN ASSOCIATION,

HARRIMAN, TENN.

105

The Cumberland Plateau

TO BE OPENED.

Arrangements have been made for opening the vast territory of the East Tennessee Land Company, on the Cumberland Plateau, by the undersigned.

FOR A CLIMATE UNSURPASSED.

FOR A HEALTHFUL HOME,

FOR DELIGHTFUL SCENERY,

GO TO THIS WONDERFUL SECTION.

Farms, Garden Spots, Town Lots in Deerment, etc., for Sale

Opportunities for Investment

AGENTS WANTED EVERYWHERE IN THIS SECTION. ALSO

ADDRESS

CUMBERLAND PLATEAU IMPROVEMENT CO.

HARRIMAN, TENN.

191